Enigma and the Bombe

by Frank Carter and John Gallehawk

CONTENTS

Introduction

The first edition of this publication was written over ten years ago, and although most of the original content has been revised and rewritten the objectives remain much the same.

In a short visit to BP it is difficult to achieve a good understanding of the problems involved in breaking an Enigma enciphered message and of the role of the bombes in this process. It is hoped that the descriptive material in this second edition is in a form that will be acceptable to a non-technical reader* and will provide a fuller account of the wartime work at BP than can be provided during the course of a walking tour.

Also included are a brief history of Enigma, and an account of the pre-war work of the Polish Cipher Bureau that formed the basis for the rapid developments that subsequently took place at Bletchley Park.

After intensive efforts over the past ten years the Bombe Re-Build project has successfully completed the construction of a Bombe now appropriately named 'Phoenix' which has pride of place in the BP museum. It is hoped that this publication will form a supplement to the information about the machine that is currently on display.

Frank Carter

John Gallehawk

July 2009

BP report No.4 'The Turing Bombe' provides more detailed technical information

The Enigma Machine

The first versions of the Enigma machine were developed as private ventures by a Berlin engineer, Dr Arthur Scherbius and one of these was exhibited at the Congress of the International Postal Union in 1923. It was offered for sale on the open market as a device that could be used by Banks and other commercial organisations to transmit confidential information over the public telegraph system in the form of cipher-text. This machine was not a commercial success, but in 1926 it was adopted by the German Government for military purposes. Its operational use was restricted to the German Navy, but later on an improved version of this machine was developed, and these more advanced machines were adopted by all three branches of the German Armed Forces, who subsequently used them extensively for military signals that were to be transmitted by wireless telegraphy. The original *'commercial'* machine was withdrawn from the market in 1933, although it is probable that some more machines of this early type (with minor modifications) were made after this.

It is of interest to note that one of the early machines was acquired by the British Government Code and Cipher School in 1927, and they found that it had certain weaknesses and was incapable of providing the high level of security that was thought necessary for military purposes.

The principal differences between the early *'commercial'* machine and the later more advanced *'military'* version was that the latter was manufactured solely for use by the German armed forces and had an additional device fitted to it known as the *'plug-board'*. This device greatly increased the security of the machine and consequently the German Authorities were confident that the messages enciphered on it were 'unbreakable'; this was a belief that they consistently maintained for a considerable period of time including all the years of the war.

The story of the years of struggle to break the military ciphers generated by means of Enigma machines is related to both the technical developments made to the machine from time to time and also to the changes that were made on several occasions in the operational procedures that were used with it. Both motivated the development of new cipher breaking techniques of increasing sophistication.

A description of the machine and how it was used:

The *'military'* Enigma machine generated a sequence of cipher-text letters from the corresponding sequence of plain-text letters that are typed on its keyboard.

When a letter key is depressed the movement closes a switch under the key and this completes an electrical circuit that lights a lamp (one on a panel of 26 lamps) to indicate the corresponding cipher-text letter. The convoluted wiring of this circuit passes through the interior of three moveable wheels or rotors, and also through the plug-board.

Every rotor has a set of 26 electrical contacts on each of its opposite sides, with a different internal arrangement of 26 wires connecting the contacts on one side to those on the other, so that when located in the machine every possible combination of the rotational positions of the three rotors will result in a different electrical circuit between the keys and the indicating lamps. The three rotors turn in a way that is somewhat like the motion of the wheels in an odometer fitted in a car, the right-hand rotor turning on by one position for each letter key pressed, and at a particular position, this turning motion causes the middle rotor to turn on by one place. In the same way at a certain position the movement of the middle rotor causes the left-hand rotor to turn on by one place. The design of the machine was such that when a key is pressed the rotors move before the switch under the key closes to complete the electrical circuit and to light one of the lamps.

The rotor orientations where the 'turn-overs' take place are determined by the positions of a notch cut into the side of the ring that is fitted round the rim of each rotor, rather like a tyre on a wheel. These rings either have the 26 letters (A – Z) or alternatively the 26 numbers (01 - 26) inscribed on them (the following exposition will assume them to be letters).

In the initial setting up of the machine each ring is made to rotate around the inner core of its rotor to a position where a chosen letter on the ring is aligned with a fixed index mark embossed on the rotor, and it is then locked at this position by a spring clip. These chosen positions are referred to collectively as the 'ring-settings' of the rotors and as the plain-text is 'typed' on the keyboard of the machine the 'turn-over' positions of the middle and left-hand rotors are determined by these settings.

The rotor 'turn-overs' have the following unexpected characteristic:- Every time a key is pressed on the Enigma machine the right-hand rotor moves on regularly by one position; once in every 26 of these moves (at the turn-over position set on the right-hand rotor) the middle rotor will also move on by one position. If this movement of the middle rotor happens to bring it to its own 'turn-over' position then it will move on again by one position when the next letter key is pressed, and also cause the left-hand rotor to advance by one position. This behaviour is known as the 'double stepping' of the middle rotor and it has the effect of reducing the cyclic period of the rotors from the expected value of 26x26x26 (= 17,576) to 26x25x26 (= 16,900).

The three rotors are placed side by side in one of the six possible arrangements. When in position, three small viewing windows allow one letter on each of the rotor rings to be visible to the operator. The rotors can then be turned by hand until the three letters chosen for the initial rotor starting positions appear in the three windows.
Then each letter of plain-text entered on the keyboard will result in the illumination of one of the lamps on the lamp panel indicating the corresponding letter of cipher, the electric current passing first though the plug-board to the rotors, and then again through the plug-board and finally to the lamp panel.

The function of the 'plug-board' is to enable additional special changes to be made to the electrical circuits connecting the keys to the lamps. For pre-selected pairs of letters this device enables exchanges to be made automatically between the letters in each pair in the electrical circuits between the keyboard and the rotors and again between the rotors and the indicating lamps.

After passing through the three rotors the electric circuits are connected to another device known as the 'reflector'; the internal wiring in this has the effect of returning the circuit back through the rotors for a second time but in the reverse direction and following a different path, returning again to the plug-board where further exchanges between the pre-selected pairs of letters are made.

The 'steckers':
The pairs of pre-selected letters that were subjected to these exchanges were known at BP as the *'stecker pairs'* ('stecker' is the German word for 'plug'). The remaining letters not paired for this purpose were said to be *'self-steckered'* or *'unsteckered'*.
During the war the standard German practice was to selected 10 pairs of letters each day, and one of the tasks at BP was to identify these 10 *'stecker pairs'* (by default the remaining six letters would be 'self-steckered').

The following diagram gives the basic structure of the complete machine.

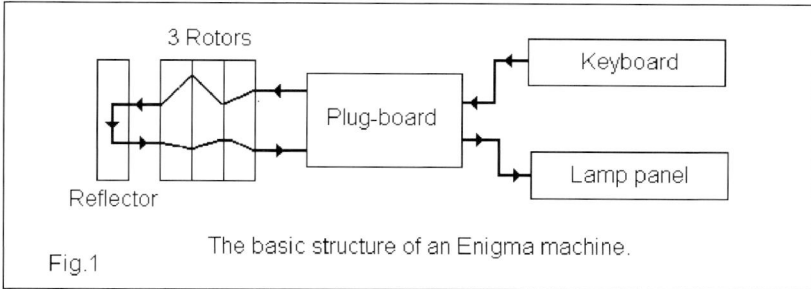

Fig.1   The basic structure of an Enigma machine.

The reciprocal characteristics of the machine:
The Enigma machine is designed to have reciprocal characteristics so that the two processes of enciphering and deciphering a message are essentially the same.
In order to understand how this can be achieved it is necessary to consider the electrical circuits inside the machine connecting the keys on the keyboard to the indicating lamps on the lamp panel. Two highly simplified versions of the circuit diagram of the machine are given showing only two of the keys and two of the indicator lamps. A machine based upon this simple circuit would be of no practical use but the electrical principles of the real machine can be readily understood by considering the characteristics of the electric circuits shown in these diagrams.

In the first diagram (fig.2) the 'stecker' pairs of letters are P/C and Q/S, and the given circuit is such that the result of pressing key 'P' is to illuminate the indicating lamp 'Q', showing that letter 'P' has been enciphered as letter 'Q'.

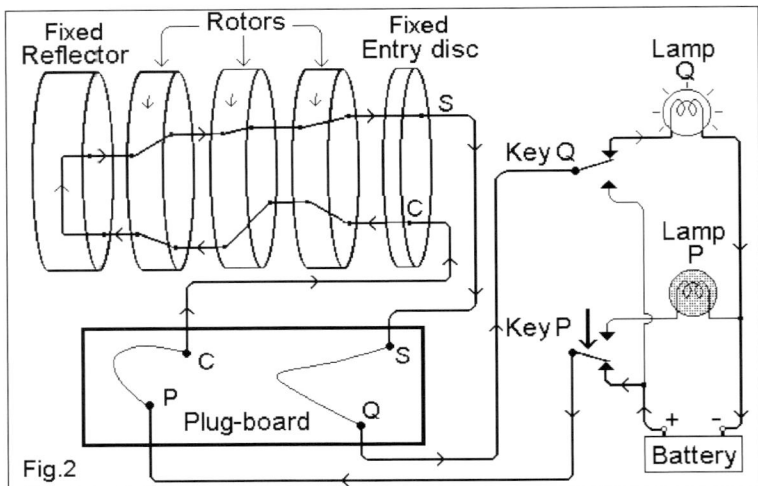

Fig.2

The second diagram (fig. 3) shows the same electrical circuit but with the key 'Q' pressed instead of key 'P', and as a consequence of the reversible nature of the electric circuit it will be seen that indicating lamp 'P' will be illuminated. So that letter 'Q' has been enciphered as letter 'P'.

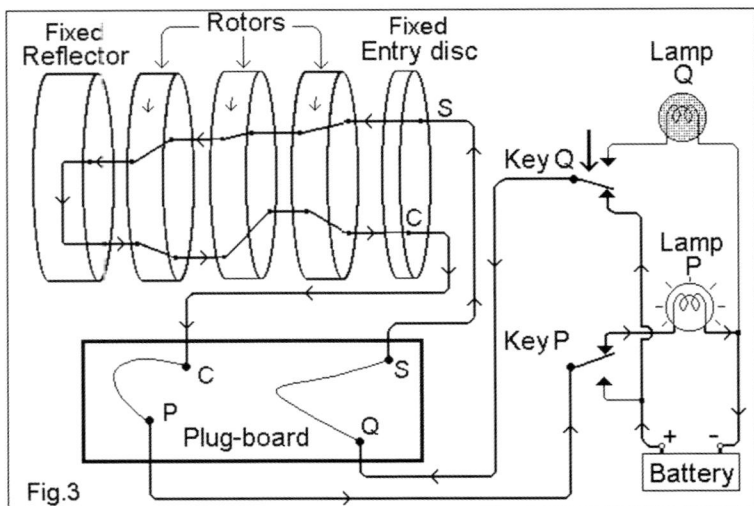

Fig.3

With the electrical circuit shown in the diagrams, the letters P and Q form a *reciprocal pair,* meaning that one of these letters will be obtained by enciphering the other. Hence if P is enciphered as Q, then at the same set of rotor positions Q will be enciphered as P. In the same way for any given configuration of the rotors, the complete machine (with 26-keys and 26 lamps) will always partition the 26-letters of the alphabet into thirteen *reciprocal pairs* of letters so that for any of these pairs one letter will always be enciphered as its partner. It has to be remembered however that when the rotors move to another set of positions the circuit configuration will alter and this will result in changes in the identity of the thirteen letter pairs, but the reciprocal relationship between the letters in each pair will remain.

The reciprocal characteristic of the machine implies that a cipher message made on one machine can be restored back to plain-text by typing it on a second machine provided that this has initially been set up in the identical way as the first one.

A weakness of the Enigma machine:

The fact that a letter will always be enciphered as its reciprocal partner in one of the letter pairs implies that no letter can ever be enciphered as itself. This was a weakness that the Germans were apparently prepared to accept for having a machine with the extremely useful property that the enciphering and deciphering processes were the same. This would have greatly simplified the training of their Enigma Operators.

The following diagram (fig 4) shows in a simplified form the wiring of the rotor system. The sliding contacts on the rotors consist of spring loaded metal pins on one side and flat metal 'plates' on the other. The diagram shows only four contacts on each side of each rotor, but actually there are twenty-six.

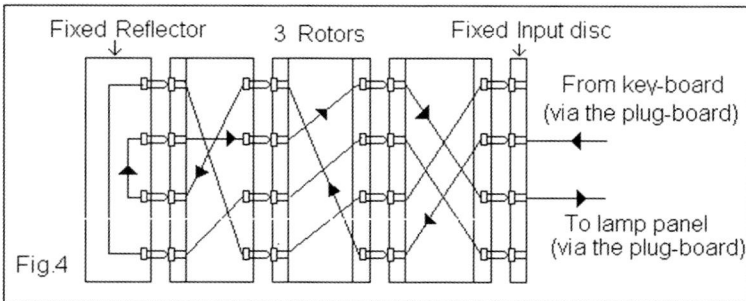

Fig.4

The Breaking of Enigma

The Pioneering work of the Polish Cipher Bureau:
This is a much abbreviated account of a long and rather complex story that began in Poland in the early 1920's:-
Colonel Lisicki who was the head of the radio unit working for General Sikorski's Chief of Staff then operating in the U.K during WW II, subsequently revealed that during the 1919-1920 conflict between Russia and Poland, radio-intelligence had played an important role in the defeat of the Russian Army in August 1920. During the Russian offensive in that summer the Polish General Staff knew from intercepted messages nearly all of the secret orders issued by Soviet General Tuhachevsky to his commanders and of the approval of them by Trotsky.
The Polish Cipher Bureau had a long tradition of interest in both German and Russian ciphers. German codes and ciphers used by the Reichswehr were successfully broken from 1918 until the introduction of the Enigma cipher machine in 1928. The Bureau purchased a *'commercial'* version of the machine and they also had scraps of information about the military version, but they were unable to penetrate the ciphers. They did however discovered from their daily lists that the sequences of the first six letters from each intercepted message had some unusual features that these must be of special significance. For example, it was discovered that for any two of these sequences of six letters if the first letter was the same in both then the fourth letters in both would also be the same.

Polish Intelligence decided to establish a cryptography course at Poznan University and invite suitably qualified candidates to apply. Three of the graduate mathematicians who were accepted to attend this course were subsequently recruited into the Polish Cipher Bureau, although at different times. Marian Rejewski who was the eldest of the three, joined the other two probably some time in late 1930. By the 1st September 1932 the Bureau had closed its office in Poznan and the members of its staff relocated in Warsaw. About one month after this Rejewski alone was set to work on the Enigma ciphers.

The early Enigma Operational Procedures:
Up until September 1938 the German military operating procedure for using the Enigma machine was as follows:- Every day, in the way prescribed in military orders, the operators placed three designated rotors into the machine in the order specified (left , middle, right). The rings on the three rotors were set to prescribed positions and the plug-board connections made according to the day's instructions (only six 'stecker' pairs were specified). The operator then turned the rotors to the prescribed positions know as the *'Grundstellung'* (i.e. *'basic rotor starting positions'*).

It is worth noting that although this operational procedure remained unchanged for several years, over that time the details varied considerably. Initially the rotor order remained the same for a period of three months and the ring-settings only changed once each month. In contrast at the end of this period both the rotor order and ring-settings was being changed every twenty-four hours at midnight. The number of stecker pairs that were used also increased during this period.

The next part of the procedure was that the Operator made his own choice of three letters forming the *'message settings'* for the message he intended to encipher and then typed these three letters twice in succession on his Enigma machine, the resulting six letters being placed before the beginning of the enciphered message when it was finally transmitted. The Operator next turned the rotors to the positions of his chosen *'message settings'*, and then proceeded to encipher the message itself on the machine.

 This procedure had two important features:-
(i) The individual *'message settings'* chosen by the Operators were all enciphered on the machine with the rotors initially set to the same *'basic starting positions'*.

(ii) The first six letters at the beginning of each transmission were the result of enciphering the three letters of the *'message settings'* twice in succession. This meant that the 1st and 4th letters of cipher both represented the first letter of the *'message settings'*. Likewise the 2nd and 5th letters of cipher both represented the second letter of the 'message settings'', and the 3rd and 6th letters of cipher both represented the third letter of the *'message settings'*.

Rejewski's recovery of the secret internal wiring of the Enigma rotors:
In his investigations on the Enigma machine Marian Rejewski exploited these two features in an outstandingly brilliant way. He has described how by means of a systematic examination of the sequences of the first six letters in all the intercepted messages on a given day, he was able to develop a procedure that made it possible to deduce the internal electrical connections of the rotor occupying the right-hand position in the Enigma machines on that day. However in order to do this it was necessary to know the plug-board connections that had been used and also the details of the electrical connections between the keyboard and the input disc on the Enigma machine.

In December 1932, at the time when Rejewski was considering possible ways of dealing with these difficulties, the Poles received a timely gift of some secret German documents containing details of the daily plug-board ('stecker') connections for a two month period. This information was supplied by the French Intelligence Service, and had been obtained from an official of the German Defence Ministry who had offered to sell information to them. With the aid of this new information Rejewski was able to make some further progress, but was still unable to deduce the connections between the keyboard and the input disc that were needed.

In the end, after some considerable time and trouble, Rejewski made an inspired guess that turned out to be correct, and so he was then able to discover all of the secrets of the electrical wiring of the Enigma machine.

The documents that the French had supplied then enabled the Poles to decrypt the Enigma messages for the two month period that they covered, and this work was carried out by Rejewski's colleagues while he was instructed to consider how further progress might be made. At the same time the Polish General Staff commissioned an electrical engineer, Antoni Palluth who was working for Polish Intelligence, to construct a number of replica Enigma machines based upon Rejewski's discoveries.

Reading the Enigma messages:
As has been graphically described by Rejewski, the Poles had advanced from a situation where they had information about some Enigma keys, but no knowledge of the machine, to one where they had all the information about the machine together with their Polish made versions of it, but no keys for the new messages they were then intercepting.

Further progress was made after the Poles had identified certain characteristics of the permutations* associated with the sets of the first six letters in all of the messages intercepted on a given day, which could be used to identify the rotor order and the basic starting positions that had been used. It followed that if a complete catalogue of these characteristics could be compiled, it could then be used to give the information required each day about the rotors. The complete catalogue would contain no less than $105,456 (= 6 \times 26 \times 26 \times 26)$ entries, and to provide this information the Poles constructed a small hand operated machine known as the 'Cyclometer', based upon Enigma rotors. The information produced by this machine was subsequently recorded in a structured card catalogue. This catalogue often enabled the rotor order, the basic starting positions, and also the 'stecker' connections to be found in about 20 minutes.

However there were some days when life was not so easy and success eluded them.

One very elegant feature of the catalogue was that the permutation characteristics used for it were independent of the plug-board connections.

New problems confronting the Poles:
The catalogue fulfilled its useful role for several years up until the 15th September 1938, when the Germans made a major change in the operation procedure. Thereafter the Operator himself chose at random the basic starting positions for each message, instead of using the one prescribed for the day as had previously been the case. As a consequence of this change the first of the two important features previously described was lost, so that the catalogue could no longer be used. However the second feature remained and it was this that was exploited in new ways.

The basic starting positions chosen for each message by the Operator were now transmitted in plain-text, but because they did not know the *'ring-settings'*, this information was of no direct use to the Poles. However it sometimes happened that in the six letters of the enciphered *'message settings'* (the nature of which has already been described), the 1st and the 4th letters would be the same, likewise sometimes the 2nd and the 5th letters and sometimes the 3rd and the 6th letters. These events did not occur very often and so they could be used as a basis for finding the rotor characteristics that had caused them to occur.

Refer to BP Report No 2 for more detailed information about permutations and the Polish work.

Both of the new methods used took the form of searches for the rotor order and the ring-settings, based upon the repetitions of the letter pairs that were found in some of the enciphered message keys in the daily intercepted signals.

The Polish 'Bomba':

One of the searching methods depended upon a small machine known as a 'Bomba' that became ready for operational use in November 1938. This was based upon six Enigma rotor systems driven by an electric motor. The machine was designed to stop when the six sets of rotors became aligned at the special positions that reproduced a pattern of repeated letters that had been found in the enciphered message settings of some of the many signals intercepted on a given day. Six of these machines were constructed and operated together to deal simultaneously with the six possible rotor orders. For the machine to achieve success it was essential that the plug-board had **not** been involved when the original repeated *'message settings'* had been enciphered on the Enigma machines. On the assumption that several hundred messages would be intercepted each day Rejewski estimated that about three enciphered 'message settings' with the required characteristics would be found every other day. However later when the Germans significantly increased the number of steckered pairs of letters to ten the effectiveness of the Bomba's (plural 'Bomby') was greatly reduced.

The Zygalski sheets:

A second method that was developed in parallel with Rejewski's 'Bomba', used sets of square sheets of thin card marked out with a complex pattern of square perforations. As each sheet had more than 1000 perforations on it and every perforation had to be made precisely at one of 2601 possible locations, much time and care was needed in their preparation. These perforations were punched at positions on the cards that represented the 'ring-settings' of messages that would have the repetitions of the letters in their indicators previously described. No attempt will be made here to explain the theory behind their use*, but in practical terms certain selected sheets were arranged on top of one another on an illuminated glass-topped table. The positions at which light passed through perforations on all of the selected sheets provided information for finding possible rotor orders and ring-settings. Sometimes with luck only one such position was found thus providing a unique solution.

These sets of card were known as 'Zygalski sheets' after the inventor, who was another of the three graduates recruited earlier in 1932. The great advantage of this method was that it was independent of the number of 'stecker' letter pairs being used and so unlike the 'Bomba' this method remained valid after the Germans had increased the number to ten.

Further difficulties:

In December 1938 the Germans introduced two additional rotors but luckily the Poles were able to discover their wiring using the same technique as they had done previously for the original three rotors, however at this juncture other serious problems presented themselves.

* The theoretical basis of Zygalski's method is given in BP report No.2 'The First Breaking of Enigma'

With the three original rotors there were six possible rotor orders to consider and only six sets of Zygalski sheets to make, although each of these sets contained twenty-six individual cards (all being made by hand!). With the introduction of two new rotors there were now sixty possible rotor orders to consider and consequently sixty sets of sheets were needed. This huge task was quite beyond the limited resources available to the Poles and subsequently the number of messages they were able to decipher was very greatly reduced. As a consequence during the critical period of the German military build up throughout the months of 1939 leading up to the campaign in Poland in September of that year the Polish High Command had little access to the German enciphered information.

The pre-war work of the G C & C S on Enigma:

In 1927 the British Government Code and Cypher School (then based in London) carried out an investigation on the *'commercial'* Enigma machine. However their main activities were then and for some years after, directed at the ciphers of the Soviet Government, and with good reason as some broken message made it evident that they were attempting to subvert the U.K. to their political philosophy. It was not until the Spanish Civil War in 1936, that the first efforts were made by GC & CS to break Enigma enciphered signals. Compared to the Poles the British were geographically at a considerable disadvantage, and only a few signals were successfully intercepted.

In 1937 a modified version of the *'commercial'* Enigma machine that had been supplied by the Germans to the Italian and Spanish Forces was broken, and this paid a dividend later in 1941 after the Italians had entered the war. The successful action by the Royal Navy against the Italian fleet off Cape Matapan was mainly due to the breaking of some Italian Naval signals that had been enciphered on Enigma machines of this type.

However there was little progress in breaking the ciphers of the more advanced versions of the Enigma machines that were fitted with a plug-board. Sometime around 1938 GC & CS acquired (probably from French Intelligence) a message enciphered on this type of machine together with the plain-text and also the details of the 'stecker' letter pairs that had been used. Initially it had been hoped that this information might be sufficient to make it possible to deduce the internal wiring of the rotors that had been used (i.e. the problem that Rejewski had solved some six years previously).
Interestingly GC & CS was subsequently confronted with the same problem that Rejewski had previously encountered (i.e. finding the connections between the keyboard and the input disc) that he solved by means of a 'lucky' intuitive guess. Unfortunately the British did not make the same guess and by July 1939 had still not solved this problem.

The Pyry meeting:

In July 1939, as Poland's contribution to the common cause, the Country's secret knowledge about the Enigma system (together with their current difficulties) was revealed to representatives from British and French Intelligence. The three British representatives were Cmd. A.G. Denniston (BP's first director), Dillyn Knox (Chief cryptographer at GC & CS) and Cmd. H. Sandwith (Admiralty radio specialist). The meetings took place in a Polish Intelligence centre situated near the village of Pyry some 6 miles south of Warsaw. Subsequently under conditions of great secrecy, two Polish made replicas of the advanced Enigma machine were transported to France (most probably by sea) and subsequently one of these was brought to London.

This machine, together with the information about Rejewski's Bomba machine and Zygalski's perforated sheets, enabled the British to fully exploit the potential of the early discoveries made by the Poles about the German military Enigma cipher system.

The early work at Bletchley Park:
Evidence shows that it is almost certain that no copies of the Polish Bomba were ever manufactured by the British as they considered that these machines were unlikely to be effective because of the current increase to ten in the number of 'stecker' letter pairs being used.

However Zygalski's method was not compromised by the increased number of 'steckers' and in August 1939 high priority was given to the massive task of making the required sixty sets of Zygalski sheets that were needed to cope with the sixty possible rotor orders resulting from the increase in the number of rotors being used with the Enigma machines from three to five. In addition to the sixty sets intended for use at BP duplicate sets were also made to give to the Polish cryptographers who were by that time working at The French Cipher Bureau situated about 23 miles S.E. of Paris. The mammoth task was completed by the end of December 1939.

Early in January 1940 following the completion of this work, Alan Turing travelled to France to meet the Polish mathematicians and to give them the newly completed duplicate sets of Zygalski sheets. After this meeting there was a relatively short period of time lasting about three months during which the joint British/Polish endeavours were rewarded with the first breaks into the Enigma traffic for over a year.

As previously stated both of the Polish methods for breaking Enigma depended critically upon the German operational practice of twice enciphering the rotor *'message settings'* and the British feared that this might be changed at any time. Consequently they were urgently seeking alternative ways of breaking Enigma that did not rely upon this operational procedure, and from the first months of the war Turing was considering alternative approaches to the problem.

Turing decided that the best way of proceeding was to develop a method that would not be invalidated by any future changes in the German operational procedures. His ideas, when combined with those of his colleague Gordon Welchman, lead to the development of a new machine known as the 'Bombe'; however it was about eight months before it came into effective operational use.

On the 1st May 1940 the Germans changed their operational procedure, and from this date the *'message settings'* were only enciphered once. This meant that the Zygalski sheets immediately became useless (with the exception for a short time of the messages transmitted from Norway). This was very nearly a disastrous blow to the British cryptographers as the Bombe was not then fully operational and they had to rely on improvised techniques that depended upon security lapses made by some of the Enigma operators. Providentially during the summer of 1940 these security lapses apparently increased in number. Some of these major difficulties were resolved by the arrival in August 1940 of the first fully operational Bombe.

The Enigma machine and the German Operational procedure 1940-45*:

During this period the German Army and Air Force Enigma Operators, following specific detailed instructions, would each day take three rotors from the five available and place them into the machine in the specified order. The 'ring-settings' of the rotors were adjusted to the positions specified, and likewise following the instructions ten *'stecker pairs'* were set up on the plug-board.

Before a message was enciphered the Operator would set (i.e. turn) the three rotors to positions such that three letters he had chosen for himself were visible in the three viewing windows on the Enigma machine.

The number of different electrical configurations of the Enigma machine that could be made in this way is extremely large, as the following analysis shows:-

Possible ways of selecting three rotors from five = 10

Possible ways of ordering the three selected rotors = 6

Possible ways of selecting ten pairs of letters (from 26) = 150 million, million

Possible ways of setting the three rotors = $26 \times 26 \times 26 = 17,576$.

The product of these four factors is equal to the number of possible ways of electrically configuring the Enigma machine before enciphering a message.

The result is approximately 158, million, million, million ($= 158 \times 10^{18}$).

(Note: The *'ring-settings'* are not involved in this calculation.)

Breaking the Enigma Cipher:

To read the plain-text for an enciphered message it was necessary to have found all of the following parts of the Enigma 'key' that had been used:-

(i)   The identity and location in the machine of the three selected rotors known as the 'rotor order'.

(ii)   The *'ring-settings'* of the rotors (these determined the positions of the 'turn-overs' of the middle and left rotors).

(iii)   The identity of the ten 'stecker' letter pairs set up on the plug-board.

(iv)   The initial positions (*'message settings'*) of the three rotors used to encipher the message.

The operation procedure used during this period of time by the Germans was to prescribe in advance for a period of one month, the daily rotor order, ring-settings, and 'stecker' pairs for each of their communication links; these instructions were issued to the Operators in the form of printed 'Setting sheets'. Part of a setting sheet is shown giving the Enigma keys for six particular days in a month:-

* The procedures used by the German Navy are described in B.P. report No. 3

Geheim!			Sonder-Maschinenschlussel										BGT				

Tag	Walzenlage			Ringstellung			Steckerverbindungen										Kenngruppen			
30	I	IV	V	13	12	10	BT	CJ	DX	EF	GY	HQ	NW	PR	SZ	UV	olv	vur	uec	zgs
29	II	III	IV	07	17	08	AO	BY	EI	HR	JS	KN	LZ	MU	PV	WX	mpn	ygd	rok	wif
28	V	II	I	17	11	03	AK	CV	DQ	EN	HB	JP	LU	MZ	TW	XZ	foz	zaw	zkq	wrg
27	IV	I	III	21	09	16	AV	BQ	EZ	FN	GU	HX	JS	MP	RY	TV	ktc	ifj	hvp	poc
2	II	IV	I	15	23	07	AD	CJ	DL	GM	IO	NP	SU	TW	SU	WZ	efr	klm	gdk	rvh
1	IV	V	III	13	04	19	AK	BR	ET	FQ	HN	LS	MU	PV	WD	XJ	fhs	chr	atw	rtv
(Day)	(Rotor order)			(Ring-settings)			(Ten plug-board connections)								(Discriminants)					

Note: The 'discriminants' were not part of the Enigma keys ; they were sometimes included in the plain-text preface of the cipher messages to enable an Enigma operator to identify those that had been enciphered on his keys and were intended for him to read, from the others that had been enciphered on different keys.

As can be seen, items (i), (ii), and (iii) from the list previously set out were given on the setting sheet for each day, these were collectively known as the *'key for the day'*. The *'message settings'* were not so prescribed and it was left to the sending Operator, having obeyed the printed instructions, to make a random choice of three letters for the *'message settings'* he intended to use.

In order to inform the receiving station of these letters, the sending Operator randomly chose another set of three letters and these were subsequently transmitted (*in clear*) to the receiving Operator; these three letters were known as the *'indicator settings'*.
The sending Operator next enciphered the three letters of his chosen *'message settings'* using the *'indicator settings'* for the rotor starting positions, the resulting three letters of cipher, known as the *'indicator'* were also transmitted together with the enciphered message to the receiving Operator.

The receiving Operator, having also followed the instructions on his printed setting sheet, would then set his Enigma rotors to the *'indicator settings'* he had received *'in clear'*, and would then type the three letters of the received *'indicator'*, thus recovering the three letters of the *'message settings'* that had to be used to decipher the message. The *indicator settings* and the *indicator* were sometimes referred to collectively as the *'indicator groups'*.

After re-setting the rotors to the recovered *'message settings'*, the Operator recovered the original plain-text by typing on the Enigma key-board the letters of the cipher-text.

The BP 'Code-Breaking' strategy:

The first objective was to find the initial orientation of the internal wiring cores of the three rotors that were referred to as the *'core starting positions'*. These were determined by the *'message settings'* and ring-settings that had been used to encipher the message, and initially both were unknown.

The strategy adopted was to begin by making the assumption that the unknown *'ring-settings'* were:- 'ZZZ'. It was of course very unlikely that these three settings were correct and the subsequent procedure was to find by means of the Bombe, the rotor settings that together with the assumed *'ring-settings'* 'ZZZ' resulted in the same rotor *'core starting positions'* as the (unknown) combination of *'message settings'* and *'ring-settings'*, that had originally been used to encipher the message. The rotor settings that were found by the Bombe were, for somewhat arcane reasons, known as the *'rod positions'*. At a later stage of the work, after the original *'ring-settings'* had been found, it was then possible to make the necessary corrections to the *'rod positions'* and to determine the original *'message settings'*.

The procedure described above is not easy to come to terms with and requires a careful explanation. A particular set of rotor *'core starting positions'* can be represented by many different pairs of rotor settings and ring-settings. For each rotor the *'core starting position'* can be represented by the 'difference' between the 'setting' letter and the *'ring-settings'* letter (i.e. the number of places in the alphabet by which they differ). Suppose for example that the *'message settings'* and ring-settings for an enciphered message are respectively JHL and DGR, when taken together these give the original rotor *'core starting positions'*. At BP both these would have been initially unknown, and the ring-settings would at first have been assumed to be ZZZ.

Then with these *'ring-settings'* it can be shown that the corresponding *'rod positions'* required for the rotors to give the original 'core starting positions' will be:- FAT.

This can be explained by means of the diagrams (fig. 5) showing just the left-hand rotor adjusted in three different ways.

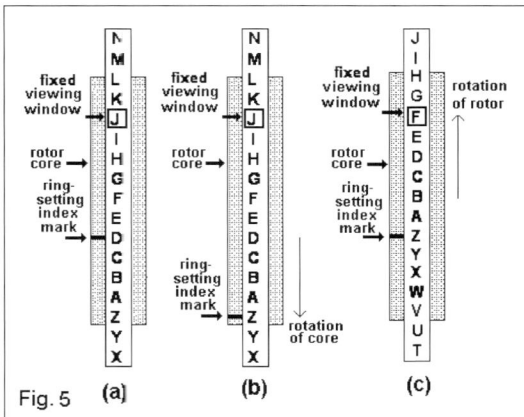

Fig. 5   (a)   (b)   (c)

In diagram (a) the rotor setting is 'J' the *'ring-settings'* is 'D' so the letter 'D' on the ring is aligned to be in registration with the index mark on the core of the rotor, and then the entire rotor has been moved so that letter 'J' appears in the left-hand viewing window on the Enigma machine. (Note: the positions of letters 'J' and 'D' in the alphabet differ by six places).

16

In diagram (b) the ring-setting has been changed from 'D' to 'Z' by turning the inner core of the rotor 'forwards' so that the index mark on it comes into registration with letter 'Z' on the ring. Note that the ring itself has not been moved and letter 'J' still appears in the left-hand viewing window.

In diagram (c) the rotor setting has be changed from 'J' to 'F' by turning the entire rotor (including the core) 'backwards' so that the letter in the viewing window changes accordingly. Note that this has the effect of moving the index mark on the core (together with the internal wiring) to their original positions. (Note: The positions of letters 'F' and 'Z' in the alphabet differ by six places.)

Similar thinking applied to the two other rotors should lead to the conclusion that rotor *'rod positions'* F A T and *'ring-settings'* ZZZ do represent the same set of rotor *'core starting positions'* as message settings JHL and *'ring-settings'* DGR

The penalty incurred by assuming the *'ring-settings'* to be ZZZ, is that the true locations of the left and middle rotor 'turn-over positions will almost certainly differ from those given by the assumed letters. During the war the correct turn-over positions had to be found by a sequence of trials that were made at the last stage of the 'code-breaking' process.

For the Bombe to produce the required outcome it was essential that the correct rotor order was being used, and usually a number of possible orders had to be tried out before the correct one was found, indeed sometimes in difficult circumstances it would be necessary to test all the sixty possible ones. However during the war various ways were found to greatly reduce this number, some based upon the discoveries made by analysis of the records that were kept of Enigma keys that had been previously broken. Often these so called 'rules of keys' resulted in a considerable reduction in the number of possible rotor orders that had to be investigated.

When taken together the 'stecker' letter pairs and the message settings involved by far the greatest number of possibilities (over 2½ million, million, million, for every rotor order) and clearly presented a major problem. The task of reducing this huge number to a value of manageable size was carried out on the Bombe.

The Rationale of the Bombe:
The initial design of the bombe was based upon the work of Alan Turing. The success of the logical procedure that this electrical machine was designed to carry out (it did not perform numerical calculations) depended upon first finding a suitable 'crib' from a cipher message. A crib consisted of the one to one matching of a short sequence of letters from the original cipher-text with those of the corresponding plain-text. As a significant proportion of the German messages were known to be 'stereotyped' (i.e. that some of the messages intercepted each day contained particular passages of text that had occurred in messages intercepted on previous days) it was possible to find cribs.

Some of the messages that were broken during the summer of 1940 as a consequence of the lapses in German security later became a valuable source of cribs when the first Bombe became operational.

An example of a crib is given below:-

Position	1	2	3	4	5	6	7	8	9	10	11	12	13	14	15	16
Cipher-text	L	V	M	F	C	C	L	U	J	Q	T	E	E	Q	E	L
Plain-text	E	I	N	X	A	B	S	T	I	M	M	S	P	R	U	Q

From the crib a diagram known as a '*menu*' can be constructed based upon the letter pairs contained in it. In this example the menu consists of eighteen letters that are linked together to form three disconnected networks, with the main network containing two closed loops.

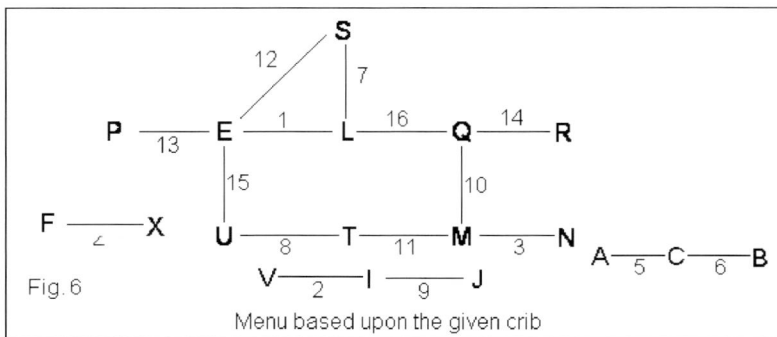

Fig. 6   Menu based upon the given crib

Before proceeding further, an explanation of the following expressions will be needed in order to understand the subsequent information relating to the Bombe:-

A **'partial key'** refers to a combination of rotor order, the '*rod positions*' of the rotors, and an incomplete set of 'stecker' letter pairs that will enable the letters of cipher-text appearing on the menu to be deciphered (but no others).

A **'complete key'** as recovered by the Bombe refers to the unique combination of Enigma rotor order, the '*rod positions*' of the rotors, and a set of ten 'stecker' letter pairs that will subsequently enable the correct decryption of the letters of cipher-text appearing in the message up to a position where a middle rotor 'turn-over' had occurred during the original enciphering of the message.

It was then necessary to discover the true original ring-settings that had been used by the German operators that day and these could be found (by some additional work) from the intercepted message '*indicator groups*'. Once the original '*ring-settings*' had been recovered, they could then be used to derive the true original *'message settings'* from the *'rod positions'* of the rotors given by the Bombe. With this additional information the entire message could then be deciphered.

How the Bombe functioned:
The fundamental theoretical work preceding the development of the Bombe had led to the following important conclusions:

(i) For a given menu there was a high level of probability that a number of alternative 'partial keys' existed, but that from one of them a complete key could subsequently be derived.

(ii) Menus with closed loops in their structure imposed a substantial limitation on the number of possible partial keys. The Bombe was designed to carry out a systematic search for the partial keys.

The practical procedure:
First an electrical circuit based upon the structure of the menu was 'plugged up' on the panel of sockets on the back of the Bombe. Then using a chosen rotor order and a particular letter from the menu selected by the Bombe operators known as the *'input letter'*, it was the function of the machine to systematically run through all of the 17,576 possible rotor core positions one by one, and to carry out an electrical test at each of them to determine if the current positions led to a logically consistent 'stecker' partner for the input letter. If a logically consistent 'stecker' partner for the *'input letter'* was found then the Bombe would stop, if not then the machine would immediately move on to the next rotor core orientation and repeat the testing procedure.

Each Bombe 'stop' provided three elements of a possible Enigma key namely the rotor order, the *'rod positions'* of the rotors (for the assumed *'ring-settings'* ZZZ), and the 'stecker' partner of the input letter that had been chosen from the menu. Each stop had to be subsequently checked further by a hand procedure that deduced from the one 'stecker' pair that had been found directly from the 'stop', the 'stecker' partners of all the other letters on the menu. (A small hand operated device known as a 'Checking Machine' was used to carry out this work) The 'stecker' pairs thus found were then examined to see if any logical inconsistencies existed between them; for example it might be discovered that two letters appeared to have the same 'stecker' partner, which was logically impossible. The 'stops' that resulted in inconsistent stecker pairs occurred as a result of random chance and were not due to technical faults on the machines.

Theoretical considerations had shown that such 'random 'stops' were to be expected, and in fact the number to be expected could be estimated quite accurately from the structure of the menus. If no such inconsistencies were found then the 'stop' was regarded as a 'good' one that would to lead to a 'partial key',

All of the partial keys identified in this way were then checked again in a different way by setting them up in turn on a British emulation of an Enigma machine and typing in some of the opening letters from the original cipher-text, the resulting sequence of letters would then be inspected for the presence of fragments of German plain-text.

When this occurred then further work, requiring linguistic skills and experience, was carried out to try to identify any remaining missing 'stecker' letter partners. Even at this late stage there was still a chance that a logical inconsistency between the 'steckers' might be found, resulting in the rejection of a promising partial key, but usually a partial key would be found that provided a 'complete key' for the message.

Finally the *'rod positions'* of the rotors and the *'ring-settings'* 'ZZZ' from the 'complete key' had to be jointly adjusted to obtain the correct rotor 'turn-over' positions as determined by the original (unknown) ring-settings. If this was not done then it would be found that after typing in some of the letters of the cipher-text on the emulation of the Enigma machine, the resulting output sequence of 'good' plain-text, would 'go wrong' at some specific position, and the letters after this would be random. After the completion of this stage of the work the original *'ring-settings'* and message settings could be found by a method that used the indicators that had appeared in the plain-text preface to the original message. Then having recovered the complete *'key for the day'* from this one message, all of the other messages sent on this key could be broken by means of the same procedure as the German Operators were using.

Additional difficulties:

The description of the process used to find an Enigma key as so far described, has avoided two additional problems that in fact made the work more difficult than it might currently appear; these were:-

(I) Very large numbers of random stops.

As has been explained it was necessary to test a number of possible rotor orders on the Bombe, and an obvious difficulty would obviously arise when the rotor order being tested was wrong, as then all of the 'stops' found by the Bombe would be random ones. At this stage of the work the Bombe operators had no insight about the validity of a 'stop', and would have reported all of them for further examination. At worst in the absence of any Intelligence information, all sixty rotor orders would have to be tested, so that ultimately the total number of stops reported could be considerable.

(II) The occurrence of Enigma middle rotor 'turn-overs'

One very important point about the process carried out with the Bombe is that the machine could not take into account the possibility that an Enigma middle rotor 'turn-over' might have occurred during the generation of the letters from the original cipher-text that had been used for the construction of the menu. Indeed the process would fail if this had happened, and so it was necessary to restrict their number to not more than about 13 letters, to reduce the chances of this misfortune occurring to no more than 50%. This necessity sometimes resulted in menus that gave an inconveniently large number of random stops.

The Diagonal Board:

An initial logistical difficulty was having to deal with the large numbers of Bombe 'stops' that occurred as a result of the necessity of using menus that had unfavourable structures. Ideally menus having at least three closures (loops) were required in order to reduce the number of 'stops' to reasonable values (about 4 stops per rotor order). However in practice it was found that the number of cribs leading to such menus was disappointingly small, and without further development the first prototype Bombe would only have been of limited use.

A remarkable example of innovative thinking on the part of the mathematician Gordon Welchman resulted in the invention of a supplementary device known as the *'Diagonal board'*. When this was incorporated into the design of the Bombe, it had the effect of dramatically reducing the number of random stops.

In effect the 'strength' of a menu no longer depended entirely on the number of loops it had, and so, for example it sometimes became feasible to use a menu with only a single loop or even in extreme circumstances with no loops at all. This meant the Bombes could be successfully used with many more cribs than would otherwise have been the case.

This is probably the best place to emphasise how effective the Turing/Welchman Bombe was. For each of the 17,576 possible 'rod positions' of the rotors there are 26 possible 'stecker' partners for the chosen input letter on the menu, (including itself). Remarkably by means of the electric circuits in the machine all of them were tested simultaneously and those not logically consistent with the other letters on the menu, rejected, the entire task being accomplished in less than 20 minutes.

Summary:
With the added power provided by the diagonal board the Bombe became a remarkably effective machine. However its success was still dependent on the availability of accurate cribs and the evidence now available makes it clear that sometimes considerable difficulties were encountered in finding them.

It appears that for the intercepted messages when no part of their keys were known, only about one in ten provided a crib that was of practical value that could be used on the Bombes, and this would seem to suggest that the proportion of messages that were broken must have been very small. However it has to be remembered that a *'key for the day'* used on an Enigma communication link remained unchanged for a period of 24 hours, and consequently during this period it was likely that a considerable number of messages would have been intercepted, thus giving a good chance that at least one of them would have provided a useful crib that would enable the key to be found.

Having found the *'key for the day'* from one message, the task of deciphering all the other messages transmitted over the same link, and for the same time period, was reduced to simply finding the message settings as all the other elements of the key would be the same as for the one message that had already been broken with the aid of the crib. If an emulation of an Enigma machine was set up to the *'key for the day'* the message settings could be found directly from the indicator setting and indicator given at the beginning of every message in the way previously described on page 15.

A question likely to arise in the mind of the reader is:- 'how were the message cribs found?' There was of course an element of luck as well as skill and accumulated experience required for success, but quite often a particular type of routine message that was transmitted just after a change of key, could be very useful. The content of the message might well have been of no value, but often it provided a readily identified crib that could be used with the Bombes to find the *'key for the day'*.

The Official History of Hut 6 refers to the regular routine transmissions of W/T test tuning messages and gives the following example:-
'DAS IST EIN ABSTIMMSPRUQ…..' . (i.e. *'This is a test message…*).
(The Archives at Bletchley Park have a small number of German Air Force messages including one (a tuning signal) that contains the expression 'ABSTIMMSPRUCH').
Clearly such messages would be a valuable source of cribs provided that they could be identified; it was often possible to do this from the call signs of the stations involved, the transmission frequencies used, the times of transmission and the length of the cipher messages.

Locating the correct position of the letters of the crib in the entire message was not always easy. One very useful fact was with any Enigma cipher no letter is ever enciphered as itself, and applying this rule greatly reduced the number of possible locations of the crib. However the Germans often inserted dummy words at the beginning of their messages to add to the security of their system and the presence of these made the task more difficult.

An Outline Description of the Engineering design of the Bombe:

The Bombe is essentially an electro-mechanical machine operating under the control of a complex system of electrical relays, designed to detect the electrical conditions required for a 'stop'. The machines were manufactured by the British Tabulating Machine Company at Letchworth, under the direction of Harold 'Doc' Keen and by the end of the war over two hundred of them were in operation.
The design of the machine was based on the equivalent of the rotor systems of thirty-six Enigma machines that were mechanically connected together and driven by a large electric motor. These were arranged in three banks of twelve on the front face of the machine, each consisting of three 'drums', which emulated the original Enigma rotors, so that the front of the Bombe carried one hundred and eight of these drums.
Each drum had a large number of wire brush electrical contacts, all of which had to be correctly adjusted to 'make' and 'break' at the same instant, without any strands of wire from any pair of adjacent brushes making contact with each other. When the Machine was in operation the drums rotated and the wire brushes made and broke their electrical contacts with the machine at the speed at which the machine ran with a maximum contact time of 20 milli-seconds.

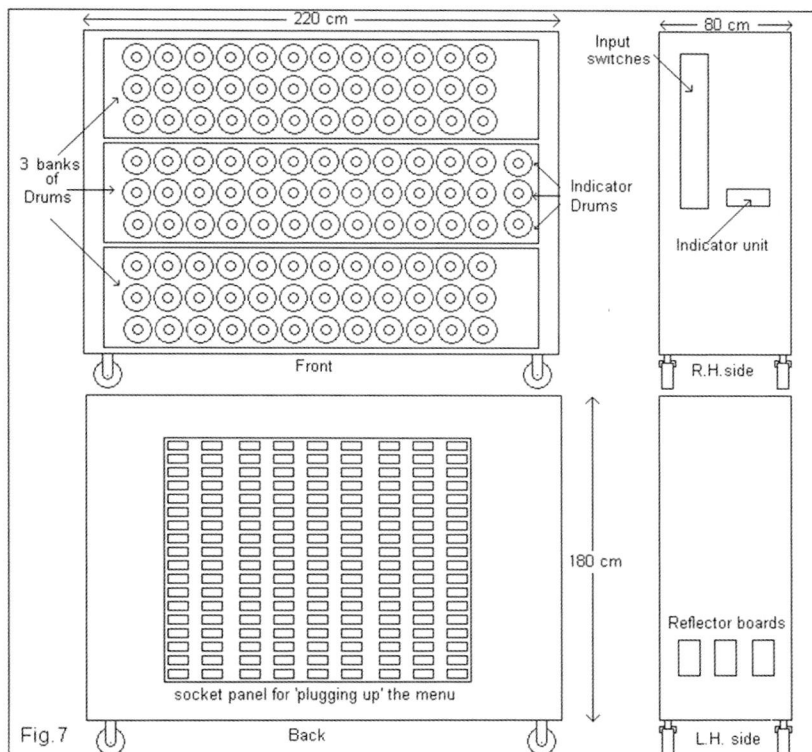

Fig. 7

On the rear face of the machine is a panel with nine columns of 26-way sockets mounted on it. These sockets are for making the electrical connections dictated by the structure of the menu and all of the connections were made by means of 26-way cables. The wiring in the Bombe was in triplicate so that the three banks of drums on the front could be set up with three different rotor orders, and the machine could be run to simultaneously test all three at the same time. The three reflector units were mounted on the left-hand end panel of the machine. Each of these units contained wiring equivalent to that in twelve Enigma reflectors. When in operation the reflectors remained fixed while the drums rotated through all of the possible setting positions. The dimensioned diagram (fig. 7) gives some indication of the size and design layout of the machine.

The rows of drums were connected to common drive shafts through systems of gear wheels, the whole being belt driven by a 0.75 H.P, D.C. electric motor

The drums were detachable and were colour coded to correspond to which of the five original Enigma rotors they emulated; for example the rotors III, II, and V corresponded respectively to the drums coloured green, maroon and yellow.

23

The drums were locked in place on the front of the machine by a latching mechanism on the face of each of them that engaged with a circumferential groove on the end of the each mounting shaft on the machine.

Once fixed in place on the machine each drum could be set by hand to any one of the twenty-six positions as prescribed by the menu. This was done by rotating each drum until the required letter on a circular scale marked on the drum was aligned against a corresponding pointer fixed to the front panel of the machine.

When in operation the middle row of drums moved on by one position after each complete revolution of the top row of 'fast' drums and likewise the bottom row of 'slow' drums moved on by one position after each complete revolution of the middle row of drums. A complete run through all 26 x 26 x26 = 17,576 positions takes approximately 20 minutes.

At each of the 'stops' found by the Bombe, the *rod positions'* defined earlier could be obtained from three special *'indicator drums'* mounted on the right-hand side of the middle bank on the machine, and the stecker letter partner of the chosen *indicator letter* was shown on the 'indicator unit' mounted on the right-hand side of the machine. This unit contained three independent sets each of 26 relays for simultaneous use with the three banks of drums. Each of the relays actuated a small indicator to display one of the letters (A –Z).

Reliability: The Bombes were expected to (and did) operate continuously 24 hours a day with no time allocated for maintenance. The first operational machine fitted with a diagonal board was in continuous use for 9 months and during that time it was only out of action for about 42 hours including the time taken to make some adaptations to it that were required for certain special jobs. It is perhaps of interest that there are some 350 lubricating points to attend to on every machine. Records from the war show that the total time for which some of the Bombes were out of action varied somewhat from 247 hours in January 1945 to only 69 hours in April of the same year, demonstrating the remarkable reliability of the machines.

All of the information given above is related to the three-rotor Enigma machines used throughout the war by the German Army and Air Force. The German Navy also used three-rotor machines but in 1942 introduced a four-rotor machine giving a higher level of security for communications with the U-boat fleet in the North Atlantic. Roughly speaking the messages enciphered with this machine were 26 times more difficult to break, or to express this in another way they would take 26 times longer to solve. This formidable cipher became known as 'Shark' and it was only after many months that BP succeeded in breaking it and then only for short periods of time with the aid of captured documents. However at a later stage of the war the problem was finally resolved by the development of 4-rotor Bombes, some in the U.K. but mainly by others developed in the United States.

Some Historical Information:

The first Bombe, given the name 'Victory', a basic design based upon Turing's original ideas and without a diagonal board arrived at Bletchley on 14th March 1940, and was located in the 'Bombe Hut' (known at the time as Hut 1). The staff assigned to operate the machine initially numbered three, one member from each of the armed services, and the machine was immediately in continuous use for 24 hours each day.

The initial work assigned to this section came from Hut 8 (Naval Intelligence). At that time the only Naval cribs available were of dubious accuracy and moreover the three rotors used in the German Naval Enigma machine were selected from a set of eight, which meant that when using the Bombe with a trial menu there were no less than 336 possible rotor orders to work through. This process took about a week to complete, and if no useful outcome was obtained, the same process would have to be started again using another possible menu and so on. It was soon realised that some radical changes were necessary if this work was to be of any assistance to the War effort.

After an intense effort on the part of the manufacturers the installation of another Bombe took place on the 8th August 1940, this machine was known as 'Agnus' and was the first to be fitted with the Welchman diagonal board. With machines of this type progress began to be made, and the section did successful work for both Hut 6 and Hut 8. One incident illustrates the difficulties encountered in those early days. A special menu was sent over to the Unit from Hut 8, and was set up on the machine, but after no less than 256 'stops' had been found all of which turned out to be 'random', the job was temporarily abandoned. Eventually, by using a different procedure after some special circuits had been added to the machine, only two 'stops' were obtained, one of which was found to be correct. (This special menu was not based upon a crib, instead it was derived from some information related to the Naval Enigma keys that had been used that day, and this had been obtained by a technique known as 'Banburismus'). This message was the first Naval Enigma cipher to be broken by the section. During 1940 these two machines assisted in the breaking of 178 messages.

In 1941 it was decided to substantially increase the number of machines and to introduce members of the W.R.N.S as the Bombe Operators. The original all male staff was now assigned the task of looking after the machines in order to maintain a high level of operational efficiency and to assist with further technical developments.

At about this time, with the prospect of a progressive increase in the number of machines coming into use, a policy of dispersal was adopted to minimise the effects of possible enemy air attacks. As a consequence a number of out-stations were established. For reasons of security these were referred to by their initials, so for example 'O.S.W.' meant 'Out-Station Wavendon', and it was here that the first machine 'Victory' was located after being returned to the makers to have diagonal boards fitted. There were further technical improvements made to some of the Bombes; at the end of March 1941 the first 'Jumbo' type was delivered. Machines of this type were capable

of carrying out the task of automatically checking all the 'stops' and the printing out the details of any *'partial keys'* that were found.
(The time taken by the machine to check a stop was about 12 seconds)

The first eight of the Wrens arrived on the 24th March 1941, and the decision to deploy them as Bombe Operators was regarded as an experiment as it was doubted that young women would be capable of undertaking this work!

By the end of 1941 there were 16 machines in operation, six at BP and five at each of the two out-stations that had by then been established. The section at BP had by this time moved to Hut 11, a robust brick built structure.

During 1942 a number of developments took place, in administration as well as the introduction of new machines and techniques. One very important change was the introduction of 'Controllers', who were Wrens particularly conversant with the Enigma cipher system and had considerable operating experience with the Bombes. It became their responsibility to delegate and supervise the process of the work. In September of that year the original machine no 1 'Victory' was withdrawn from operations but was retained for experimental and instructional purposes that continued up until the end of the War in Europe. By the end of the year the number of machines had been increased to 49 and by this time four out-stations had been established. The total number of staff was now 630 including 571 Wrens, and over 5770 tasks had been run on the Bombes.

In March 1943 an important development was the delivery to the out-station at Stanmore of two high speed 4-rotor Bombes. One of these, known as the 'Keene' type from the name of the inventor, was equipped with sets of four drums, the other type Designed by Dr Wyn-Williams and known as the 'W.W' type was basically a standard three-drum machine that was coupled by a snake-like cable to an disc shaped attachment that led to the whole thing being known as a 'Cobra'.

Both of these machines were intended for work on the cipher messages produced on the 4-rotor enigma machines then currently being used by the German Navy. The rotational speed of the 'ultra-fast' fourth drums on these high speed Bombes was approximately 26 times faster than the 'fast' rotor on a standard machine (about 800 RPM). It is believed that a total of 59 British high speed Bombes were manufactured.

The British high speed Bombes were prone to some mechanical problems and were not as reliable as the standard machines; consequently they failed to meet operational requirements. In July 1943 the high speed Bombes developed in America had their first success and as the number of these machines rapidly increased the responsibility for breaking *'Shark'* passed to the United States.

Throughout the War Bletchley Park and the out-stations were never attacked by the German Air Force, although some stray bombs did fall in the Park in 1941 the damage was very slight. On February 19th 1944 incendiary bombs fell on the Wrens side of the Out-station at Eastcote and later that year on the 18th December a 'flying bomb' fell at Stanmore, about 120 yards from the working block of the Outstation . The blast walls shielded the 160 Wrens and 20 RAF personnel working there at the time.

The Bombe section was definitely a combined services operation, and this was extended in March 1944 to train United States servicemen from the 6812 Signal Security Detachment, in the work. A special 'USA' bay was established in the Out-station at Eastcote that was equipped with ten British Bombes but run entirely by U.S. servicemen. Each of these Bombes was named after a prominent city in the U.S. and the newly completed rebuilt Bombe now exhibited in Bletchley Park has been modelled on one of these British Bombes originally called 'Atlanta'.

Over the period 1940 -45 the Bombe section had grown very rapidly both in terms of the number of machines and personnel, so that by May 1945 it consisted of nearly 2000 staff of which more than sixteen hundred were Wren Operators.

The total number of operational Bombes of all types in the section then totalled two hundred and sixteen.

A 3-rotor 'Military' Enigma machine with plug-board

Interior showing the lamps, rotors and reflector (type B)